HistoryC:

The *Real* Mic

A History of the E~~xpatriate Writers in~~
Paris That Made Up the Lost Generation
By Paul Brody

■BŌŌKCAPS

BookCaps™ Study Guides
www.bookcaps.com

Table of Contents

About HistoryCaps

HistoryCaps is an imprint of BookCaps™ Study Guides. With each book, a brief period of history is recapped. We publish a wide array of topics (from baseball and music to science and philosophy), so check our growing catalogue regularly (**www.bookcaps.com**) to see our newest books.

Introduction

The collection of expatriate artists who gathered in Paris following the Great War was a diverse group, representing various backgrounds, occupations and nationalities. They were ambulance drivers, war correspondents, common trench soldiers and decorated leaders. They were also nurses, teachers, political radicals and salon proprietors. Some were too young to fight and became the stay-at-homes, feeling perhaps that the Great Event of their generation had passed them by. Some were pacifists and denounced the senseless killing created by production line warfare. This group of young artists, most of them born between 1895 and 1900, would become known as the Lost Generation. In 1920s, Paris, they were all between 20 and 30 years old and eager to test the boundaries of life. A passion for the arts, especially literature, united them under a common cause. In all their guises, the Lost Generation shared another thing – they experienced firsthand the seismic shift in culture that signaled the painful birth of the Modern World.

The Great War (1914-1918) – no one knew then it would be the first of two – transformed the world in ways that no one fully understood at the time. Perceptive individuals shared the not quite intelligible feeling that something had gone terribly wrong and would never again be right. The Great War was the first war in history to be fought primarily by the middle class. Some of the most promising young writers of the generation, including the English poets Wilfred Owen and Rupert Brooke, perished during the combat. Frustration, disillusionment and a profound sense of loss came to characterize the war-weary survivors and influenced their artistic productions.

A return to the past, however impossible, was the yearning of many artists and intellectuals. Paris, a city so perilously close to the war, became a refuge for artists throughout the 1920s. The climate of intellectual freedom and experimentation was unlike anywhere else in the Western world. Paris also held on to Old World charms, with quiet streets seemingly unchanged since the last century. It was an age before the automobile had taken over the streets, and the romantic image of Paris became a cliche marketing gimmick.

Thousands of expatriates from America and every corner of Europe flocked to the city on the Seine, eager to experiment with new artistic forms and share new ideas. In coffeehouses and salons, bookshops and publishing houses, young writers and artists debated the meaning of life and art in a changed, some would say broken, world. The Left Bank of the Seine River became an outpost for an entire generation of the dispossessed and disillusioned.

American soldiers returning from the battlefields of Europe found a home front that in some ways had changed drastically and in others stayed the same. Prohibition, more properly known as the Volstead Act, banned the production and sale of alcohol. The "Noble Experiment" felt like a slap in the face for those returning from the trauma of trench warfare. The puritanical, conservative value system of America was stifling after the soldiers' experience in Europe. At the same time, corruption at all levels of government was commonplace. Young men who had fought for an uncertain cause felt equally uncertain about their place in modern America. An exodus was, therefore, underway, led by artists and intellectuals, in search of less restrictive intellectual climates.

Chapter 1: The Great War

As the first modern war, the first war to see the full-scale deployment of machine guns, heavy artillery and chemical weapons, the Great War was poised from the outset to generate casualty counts beyond imagination. The assassination of Archduke Franz Ferdinand of Austria by a radical Serbian student, seemingly an isolated act of political terrorism, precipitated the war. Prior to the conflict, Europe had enjoyed decades of relative peace and stability. This stability resulted from a series of mutual defense pacts that deterred nations from seeking military solutions to disagreements with their neighbors. Additionally, the experience of so many years of peace led to a citizenry across Europe that became naive about warfare. In the first days of the war, cheering crowds gathered at rail stations to see their young men depart for battlefields of honor and glory. It was late summer, 1914, and no one foresaw the carnage that was to come. Nor did anyone imagine that the war would drag on for four long years.

Although peace had reigned in Europe for a generation, the technology of warfare was not stagnant. New guns, new artillery and new weaponry all vastly increased the lethality of armed conflict. The Great War was the first mechanized war and would become a prototype of every war thereafter. On the other hand, the technology of defense and mobility had remained unchanged, as had the methodology of combat. Troop movements quickly came to a halt, and the conflict degenerated into the trench warfare so synonymous with the Great War. Soldiers described the day-to-day fighting as "death on the production line" (Cowley 4). To peak one's head out of the trench was to risk death from a sniper's bullet. Ill-conceived charges through "No Man's Land" were suicide missions, and everyone knew it. Poison gas attacks struck fear into troops on both sides. Though gas attacks were strategically unimportant, their psychological effects were undeniable. Some historians have described a sort of "death wish" culture, where young soldiers embraced the futility and fatality of trench warfare. On the home front, the repercussions of the fighting would resonate for decades.

Every nation that sent troops to the front suffered mass casualties. France lost nearly 1.5 million soldiers. The United Kingdom lost more than 800 thousand. When one includes civilian deaths, the toll is even higher. Starvation, mass killings and Spanish influenza all wreaked havoc on civilian populations. Russia, for example, lost approximately 3.5 million people to the war, either directly or indirectly. The small nation of Serbia may have seen fewer absolute casualties, but as a percentage of population, the cost was nearly unfathomable: 16 percent of Serbians died in World War I. Many hoped that the Great War would be the last in history, a "war to end all wars." It was partially this hope that encouraged the United States to enter the battlefield in 1917.

As a latecomer to the fighting, the United States suffered fewer casualties than her allies. The poet Alan Seeger, a native of New York, fought and died in the French Foreign Legion, joining other famous war poets such as Rupert Brooke and Wilfred Owen. Nevertheless, the effects of war on the national psyche were profound and long lasting. Despite public approval of the war declaration against Germany, there remained a strong undercurrent of opposition to wars and other foreign entanglements. The horrific devastation of Europe and the uncertain peace following the armistice confirmed the fears of American isolationists. President Woodrow Wilson remained enthusiastic about the chances for a League of Nations to prevent future warfare; a defiant congress, however, voted against America's inclusion in the newly created international body.

The Armistice of 11 November 1918 marked the end of fighting. However, the Treaty of Versailles, signed the next year, sowed seeds of bitterness in the defeated nations – particularly Germany – that would fuel the next war. The victorious nations saw in the treaty negotiations an opportunity to deliver punishment to Germany and the other Central Powers; they took full advantage of that opportunity. There was little discussion concerning the issues that precipitated the conflict. In fewer than 20 years, national armies would once again loose destruction upon the European continent, swiftly undoing the fragile peace.

An Uncertain Homecoming

The events of 1914-1918 had profound effects at every level of society. Those nations most invested in the fighting lost thousands and millions of promising young people. Four empires crumbled while the map of Europe was forever altered. The world economy suffered a profound blow. Many nations were plagued with bankruptcy, inflation and a flood of shell-shocked war veterans. A spell of innocence and calm had been broken – an indefinable something was lost, never to be recovered. Everyone struggled to make sense of the new world and, if possible, extract meaning from the violence of the war.

In the United States, a perfect storm of circumstances created an environment that seemed almost alien to those returning from Europe. Prohibition had become the law of the land, yet organized crime and the political machine appeared to walk in lock step. Conservative values dictated the status quo, censoring artistic productions and regulating personal conduct. Artists, especially the avant-garde, had few opportunities to bring their work to a large audience. The laws regarding decency in artistic works were strictly enforced. Anything considered lewd, immoral or un-American would quickly be removed from libraries. The overall climate meant that young artists pushing the limits of their craft were locked out of the establishment.

In both Europe and America, members of the younger generation carried an unspoken grudge against their parents' generation and their value system. While this may be typical of all young people since time immemorial, those who had just emerged from a devastating world war felt perfectly justified in their misgivings. Young people in every war-torn nation questioned the institutions and belief systems that allowed such epic death and horror to take place. They questioned governments, religions, leaders and artists. They strongly questioned the blind, fanatical sense of national loyalty that allowed such unprecedented bloodshed to continue for so long. Ultimately, the young thinkers and artists of the Lost Generation would declare the "old regime" morally bankrupt and attempt to construct a new one in its place. The construction project would begin in Paris, a birthplace of brilliant and powerful ideas for centuries.

Chapter2: Paris in the 1920s

Paris became a beacon for the young and disaffected all over the world. Expatriates were drawn to Paris more so than any other European city. This was not surprising; for decades, Paris had been "the center of a gravitational pull of international artistic talent" (Fitch 16). Aspiring writers and visual artists looked to the city as the "cultural capital" of the Western World. In the 1920s, the aesthetic and cultural gulf between the United States and Paris was as wide as it had ever been. On one side of the Atlantic, the government in Washington was once more isolating the nation from foreign affairs and attempting to regulate individual behavior. On the other side, Parisians, despite the ravages of war, still lived a permissive, individualistic lifestyle that harkened back to the previous century. The climate in America was simply unsuitable for artistic inspiration and expression. Those who had already been there knew Paris was the place to be.

Two other factors encouraged the artistic migration to Paris. One was a highly favorable exchange rate. Americans could afford to live comfortably in France on a relatively small income. Those with a small nest egg and some artistic talents supported themselves reasonably well. Another factor that encouraged the exodus was inexpensive travel. In 1924, the steamship companies introduced a new ticket class that made the transatlantic journey affordable to nearly everyone. Almost immediately, a flood of intrepid travelers boarded ships for the Old World. Some tasted life in Paris for only a few days or weeks before moving on. Others fell so in love with the city that they stayed for years. Those with the weakest connections to the States often set up permanent residences, rarely to return home.

Surprisingly, it was not city dwellers, but rather Midwesterners who largely filled the ranks of the American expatriate class. In the American Midwest, the restrictive, puritanical value system had its firmest foundation. A young man from Minnesota or Missouri would have an eyeopening experience in Europe. Once home, it was difficult to readjust to the old mode of living. War veterans who had served in France already had a certain familiarity with the cafes and back alleys of the French capital. Soldiers and support personnel on leave from the Western Front often spent weekends in the city, enjoying the many charms of Parisian life. Americans often found their hometowns drab and provincial after only a few days or weeks in Paris.

Salons, Cafés and Bookshops

Street life in Paris was the ideal incubator for artistic talent. For at least two centuries, the French capital had been acknowledged as a cradle for the arts and creativity. The social and commercial life of Paris in the 1920s was inexorably tied to its reputation as a haven for artists and intellectuals. Nowhere was this more obvious than in the alleys and boulevards of the Sixth Arrondissement on the Left Bank of the Seine.

Among the oldest neighborhoods in Paris, the Sixth Arrondissement was home to Sylvia Beach's Shakespeare and Company, a lending library and bookshop that would become a focal point for the Lost Generation's literary revolution. Opened on November 17, 1919 on the Rue de l'Odéon, Shakespeare and Company would quietly bridge the gap between French, English and American readers and writers. Beach made a life for herself in France that would never have been possible in the States. She walked around the city alone, had a wide social circle, smoked and drank, and never married. Her bookstore remained open for more than 20 years and was a magnet for some of the biggest names in the literary world.

The salons were another vital aspect of cultured life in Paris. A centuries-old tradition, the salon was simply a gathering of like-minded people in a locale, usually a private residence. Gertrude Stein's Saturday evening salons, for example, were significant events for many expatriates living in Paris between the wars and provided a meeting place for individuals from diverse backgrounds. The purpose of the salon was partly to entertain and partly to educate the guests. By sharing ideas and debating philosophical points, artists found new inspiration for their work. The salon existed in opposition to university lecture halls. Guests believed that knowledge and culture could both be enhanced via intelligent dialogue.

By the mid-1920s, the Left Bank was a community unto itself. Cafes along the boulevard Montparnasse were crowded with established and aspiring artists. Joining them were journalists, admirers and literary tourists. The expatriates leased small apartments on the cheap, owing to the favorable exchange rate. Hemingway, for instance, rented one apartment for his family and another for typing his manuscripts and news stories. The atmosphere was heady. One could find a party with relative ease on any day of the week. However, it wouldn't be fair to say that the Lost Generation was hedonistic or irresponsible. As a whole, the various writers of the group maintained high levels of productivity and creativity throughout the turbulent twenties.

The Arts in Paris

The war was undoubtedly the most profound and inescapable influence on writers in the 1920s. But it was far from the only influence. Social, political and aesthetic developments were percolating throughout the first part of the 20th century. In Paris, these influences coalesced in an environment that encouraged rather than stifled their growth. The French capital was ideally situated during the war – close enough to feel threatened, even shelled on occasion but never overrun by German forces. Citizens and expatriates, especially those who had fought in the war, had the sense that Paris had only barely survived something awful.

The visual arts experienced tectonic shifts in style during this period. Pablo Picasso rode on the crest of the Modern Art wave. Several related movements signified the change in aesthetic principles. Picasso originated what became known as Cubism. More than just abstraction, Cubism involved the fracturing and rearranging of images, echoing the process of human memory and thought. Dadaism and Surrealism, both contemporary with Cubism, were challenging the long-accepted definitions of art and beauty. One of the founders of the Dada movement, Louis Aragon, argued that art with an overt, intelligible meaning was the work of a journalist, not an artist. Whereas Dadaism celebrated the absurdness of everyday objects, Surrealism elevated dreamlike imagery to a place of emotional and thematic power. These visual arts movements all owed a debt to the burgeoning field of psychology, which revealed the multilayered and complex nature of human consciousness.

Modernism in art contributed to the new and challenging literary styles that were emerging in Paris and throughout Europe. The elegant Victorian narratives that almost exclusively dealt with the middle and upper classes were seen as relics of a frivolous past. The new generation of writers believed that the elaborate language so typical of 19th century literature was a decadence. Young writers such as Ernest Hemingway and Sherwood Anderson envisioned a new narrative style and self-consciously distanced themselves from the former literary elites. Littleknown talents like James Joyce, working in obscurity as a teacher in Italy, soon found an audience for their creations.

Poetry also participated in the aesthetic revolution. In fact, poetry entered the modern age somewhat ahead of fiction and the novel. Ezra Pound, the American expatriate poet, spearheaded a movement known as Imagism. The Imagists, who included Amy Lowell, Wallace Stevens, and Hilda Doolittle among their ranks were in practice a diffuse grouping with relatively few traits in common. What Imagists did share was a belief in the power of poetry to convey distinct, powerful images. Pound especially felt that strong poetry needed a hard edge rather than flowery adjectives and exaggerated sentiments.

The confluence of so many new and unexpected artistic philosophies made for a heady brew for anyone coming to the city. The edgy, straightforward and deceptively unassuming poetry of the Imagists made a lasting impression on those who found beauty in language. Meanwhile, the new surrealist styles of art provided a window into the revolutionary world of the avant-garde. These influences encouraged writers to test new styles, new themes and new forms. From the journalistic, tough prose of Hemingway to the musical but nonsensical word poetry of Gertrude Stein, the Lost Generation was unafraid to take risks.

Chapter 3: The End of the Lost Generation

The global economic collapse of the early 1930s marked the end of typical expatriate life. The cost of living in France, or anywhere abroad for that matter, was no longer sustainable. In many cases, desperate families back home needed financial help. The Great Depression was setting in, and people everywhere were feeling desperation and fear. The independent and carefree life of the artist could no longer be seriously contemplated. Expatriate artists left the Left Bank in Paris just as quickly as they had arrived. By 1933, the community was totally broken up, and only a few hardy stragglers remained. James Joyce and Gertrude Stein were among those who stayed behind, but no longer was there a sense of togetherness and shared purpose.

Political realities also forced the hand of the Lost Generation. The mood on the continent was changing – bitterness over the previous war was quickly building toward a renewed conflict. Animosities were running particularly high. Nationalism, which many had hoped was defunct after the first war, was once more becoming a powerful factor in geopolitics. Individual artists had various responses to the changing times, further dividing an already divided creative community. Some, like Ezra Pound, identified with the fascist worldview. Hemingway, for his part, sympathized with people's revolutions in Spain and elsewhere. Others moved to the right on the political spectrum. There's an old saying the "young radicals become old conservatives," and this was certainly true for many of the Lost Generation.

Artistically, the ties that held together the artists in Paris became gradually weaker. Some had attained the height of their talent and never again produced "great" work. F. Scott Fitzgerald consummated his artistic potential with *The Great Gatsby* and never again wrote a novel on the same level of quality and importance. Some merely drifted away from artistic endeavors, pursuing professional careers instead. Others suffered early deaths or mental breakdowns. Even those who continued writing for a living saw their styles change with time. Hemingway never truly replicated the staccato style of *In Our Time* or *The Sun Also Rises*; Eliot abandoned the bleakness of *The Waste Land* and "The Hollow Men." Modernism, as a description of the literature, came to mean many different things to many people. It could no longer be neatly contained.

The Lost Generation was instrumental in wrestling literature away from the starched and formal establishment of the late 19th and early 20th centuries. The writers living in Paris in the 1920s opened a door to unexplored creative possibilities. In the post-war years, the interplay between despair and hope, fame and anonymity, and life and death was vividly enacted in the form of revolutionary literature. The Lost Generation informed and shaped all literature that would come after it, and continues to do so.

Chapter 4: Forerunners of the Lost Generation

T. S. Eliot: Poetry and Academia

Thomas Stearns Eliot was not an expatriate in the usual sense. He did not join his cohorts in Paris after the war, nor did he move in a wide social circle. Whether by choice or circumstance, he was a relatively self-contained genius. Born in 1888 in St. Louis, Eliot was attending university in England when the war broke out. Throughout the 1920s, he held various teaching positions in England, eventually becoming a citizen of that nation in 1927. Although he was and is the poster child of Modernism, his relationship with the artistic community in Paris and elsewhere was lukewarm at best.

Eliot's first published poem, "The Love Song of J. Alfred Prufrock," was a signal to the world that a new talent had arrived. The poem took a sharp turn away from the lyrical poetry of the first decade of the 1900s. "Prufrock" displayed all of the traits that would later be identified as modernist: ambiguity, moodiness, mythical allusions, stream of consciousness and despair. The first few lines of the poem were shocking at the time, as the disturbing imagery of a corpselike, "etherized" body on a table made a mockery of earlier, "prettier" poetic styles. Eliot's vast knowledge shines through in "Prufrock," as it would in all of his later productions. In fact, it was Eliot's erudition that earned him criticism from some of his fellow artists, particularly those in Paris. Some members of the Lost Generation felt that poetry and prose rightly belonged to the people and should speak with the voice of the people. They feared Eliot was stealing the art form back on behalf of "the Academy."

Whether or not the critiques of Eliot and his work were fair is remains an open question. What can't be denied, however, is the impact that his later creations would have on young artists on both sides of the Atlantic. In 1922, Eliot published *The Waste Land* in the British literary journal The Criterion. The work became a blueprint for a certain strain of Modernism that favored dense mythology, rich allusions, mystery, primitivism and darkness. Eliot was then struggling with a great deal in his personal life, thereby fueling much of the emotion evident in *The Waste Land*. However, the poem managed to transcend the personal and become universal. The sprawling, five-part, 434-line poem underwent substantial editing from Eliot's friend Ezra Pound, who cut out large sections. Noteworthy also for its vivid stream of consciousness style, *The Waste Land* shifts from serious to ironic, funny to maudlin, and displays a complex but not obvious structure. Critics once again lamented that Eliot's poetry was too dense and too proud of itself.

In spite of settling in London rather than Paris, Eliot did have something deeper in common with the Lost Generation – a complex but ultimately reverential feeling toward America. Eliot himself claimed that had he not been born in St. Louis and grown up beside the Mississippi River, he could never have produced his style of poetry and literary criticism. The combination of American roots and adult experiences of the Old World created the perfect internal environment for new ideas and inspirations. Furthermore, Eliot might never have achieved the level of recognition that he did, were it not for his friendships with, among others, Conrad Aiken, Ezra Pound and James Joyce. His small but close circle of associates was instrumental in helping him overcome both personal and professional obstacles.

Ezra Pound: The Great Promoter

Born in the Idaho Territory of the still untamed Western frontier, Ezra Pound knew from an early age that poetry was his calling. He attended Quaker schools during childhood; at age 13, his mother took him on a grand tour of Europe. He later moved east to attend the University of Pennsylvania, where he flaunted degree requirements in his quest for absolute knowledge of poetic forms in every language. His larger-than-life personality, magnetic charm, rejection of authority and obsessive tendencies foreshadowed the mental illness that plagued his later years. The memory of his tour of Europe never left him, and in 1908, Pound returned to England in a semipermanent sense.

The literary historian Hugh Kenner referred to the years 1910 to 1925 as the "Pound Era," a testament to the influence that the fiercely intelligent American poet had on his contemporaries. Pound's contributions to modern literature take several forms. On the one hand, his theories on poetry, broadly referred to as Imagism, dominated the form for many years. Imagism would strongly influence both the poetry and prose of the 1920s. Pound was also enormously successful in finding and advancing the interests of promising artists. He almost single-handedly brought fame and recognition for James Joyce, T. S. Eliot and Robert Frost. For Eliot, he published "The Love Song of J. Alfred Prufrock," and for Joyce he published a serialized version of Ulysses. He had the means and the ambition to see other renowned artists earn the praise he thought they deserved.

The First World War was a shock for Pound. Although he didn't see combat, the unfathomable loss of life caused him to question his natural affection for England. He had trouble understanding how a supposedly modern and civilized society could instigate such atrocities. By the 1930s, Pound had adopted a disturbing political stance. Namely, he supported the aims of fascist Italy and Nazi Germany. On behalf of the Mussolini regime, he recorded anti-American, anti-Semitic radio broadcasts. In hindsight, critics believe that Pound was in the early stages of a mental breakdown. His imprisonment by allied forces in 1945 pushed him over the edge and he never entirely recovered.

Despite his mental illness and questionable politics, Pound's work cannot be overestimated. Several of his poetic works are properly classified as masterpieces of the Modernist movement in literature. Among them are *Ripostes*, *Hugh Selwyn Mauberly*, and *The Cantos* – an epic poem on which he worked for most of his life. For many young writers of the Lost Generation, Pound was a powerful and persistent ally and true friend.

Gertrude Stein: Matriarch of Montparnasse

As perhaps the most enigmatic figure of 1920s Paris, Gertrude Stein filled the role of matriarch and advocate for the Lost Generation. She worked tirelessly to see that promising young artists achieved the recognition they deserved. Likewise, she loaned money to those who were literally starving for their art. Stein allegedly originated the term "Lost Generation," but several versions of the story have been put forward. The most common one outlines a conversation with Ernest Hemingway, in which she recalled a remark that her mechanic had made – he called his assistant a member of a lost generation, referring to his clumsiness. Stein borrowed the phrase, applying it to Hemingway and his cohort of expatriate writers.

Gertrude Stein was born to well-to-do German Jewish parents, in Pennsylvania. At the age of three, her cosmopolitan parents moved the family to Vienna, Italy. In 1878, they returned to the states and settled in Oakland, California. Intellectually curious from a young age, Stein studied psychology at Radcliffe College and medicine at Johns Hopkins University. Stein left the academic world behind and came to Paris in 1903, sharing an apartment with her brother Leo. The street address, 27 Rue de Fleurus, would become a famous destination for aspiring artists. In Paris, she turned her attention fully upon modern art and assembled an impressive collection of paintings, including Renoir, Matisse and Cézanne. She became locally known as an expert on modern art movements and was an early champion of Picasso. Journalists in New York contributed to the spread of her fame stateside, and Stein became a household name among the literary and cultural elite.

Stein met her life partner, Alice B. Toklas, in 1907. Although the two were quite different in temperament, everyone agreed that they complemented each other well. Stein was bold, outgoing and almost childlike, while Toklas carried herself with regal dignity. According to Ernest Hemingway, Toklas held the position of "wife" in their relationship. Stein worked quietly and subtly to advance the standing of homosexuals. In Paris, she had the privilege of living with her partner openly; in the United States, such an arrangement might have caused a scandal. Nevertheless, Stein was guarded and secretive about her sexual identity and sexual politics. Modern feminists have had a difficult time piecing together Stein's ideology. She undoubtedly holds a position as a successful woman, achieving more than most could in her day and age. However, she maintained the belief that true genius resided in masculinity as evidenced by her exclusive patronage of male artists. Some have suggested that Stein herself sought to elevate her own masculinity while debasing anything feminine in her nature. Paris in the 1920s was a suitable environment to grapple with these internal identity struggles. Countless other artists did precisely the same.

More than anything, Stein's uncanny ability to identify and nurture artistic talent was her defining contribution to the Lost Generation. She was a mentor to dozens of young writers and artists. She recognized the genius of Ernest Hemingway before he had published his first novel. Ezra Pound, Thornton Wilder and Sherwood Anderson were among the most frequent guests at 27 Rue de Fleurus. Stein's salon exemplifies one of the prominent characteristics of the Lost Generation – namely, the desire to meet, socialize, share ideas and read each other's works. Artistic partnerships were commonplace: Pound edited Eliot, Fitzgerald edited Hemingway, and so on. The Lost Generation had solidarity of purpose, not only because they frequented the same locales, but also because they saw the world through a similar lens. Informal parties with Stein and Toklas hosting helped develop this solidarity.

Although she wrote extensively and had a healthy opinion of her talents, publication was difficult for Stein. Her "word poems," which eschewed traditional concepts of meaning and narrative, were simply too removed from the mainstream for even the most daring publishers. Instead, Stein turned to the "little" magazines – small operations with few subscribers – as a means to disseminate her work. She also let much of her work go unpublished, instead collecting stacks of manuscript pages in a cabinet. Her most commercially successful work was *The Autobiography of Alice B. Toklas*, which, in signature Gertrude Stein fashion, was not, in fact, an autobiography but a personal memoir told from the perspective of Toklas.

James Joyce: The Irish Bard

The son of a middle-class Dublin family, James Joyce's fictional works always took place within the city of his birth. Joyce was the oldest of ten children. His father was a tax collector, and the family moved from the city to the outlying town of Bray in 1887. By 1893, Joyce's father had been dismissed from his position and the family began a slow descent into poverty. The elder Joyce's heavy drinking contributed to the general situation. At some point, James Joyce lost touch with his Catholic roots, although biographers disagree on the exact nature and timing of his falling out.

In 1898, at the age of 16, Joyce enrolled at University College Dublin. He studied Italian, French and English. It was during his time there that he became more involved in both theater and literature. He wrote and published several review articles and at least two plays. Joyce graduated in 1903 and went on to study medicine in Paris, but never completed that degree. The family's difficult financial situation and his mother's cancer compelled him to return home. For several years, Joyce managed to earn a living, just barely, from teaching and writing. His alcohol consumption had increased substantially, and he suffered from profound depression.

Joyce eloped to the continent with a young woman named Nora Barnacle. He sought teaching positions in several European cities, finally settling in Trieste, then part of Austria-Hungary. He taught English in the port city for nearly ten years. Joyce still suffered from bouts of excessive drinking and the urge to keep moving – he spent a year in Rome before deciding that Trieste was preferable – but he was working harder on publishing his own work. He was trying to publish his short story collection, *Dubliners*, but faced rejection at every turn. After an unsuccessful trip to his birthplace to speak with the publisher George Roberts, he never again returned to Ireland.

Dubliners was finally published in 1914, nearly 8 years after its completion. The short stories displayed the elements that would come to signify the work of James Joyce: a strong sense of time and place, richly detailed characters, interior monologue and stream of consciousness writing. Joyce began work on a novel in that same year, hoping to complete the work before his 40th birthday in 1922. The American poet, Ezra Pound, published the novel, *Ulysses*, in serial form beginning in 1918. Though he didn't realize it at the time, his fame as an avant-garde writer was beginning to grow. Pound invited Joyce to visit him in Paris in 1920. Rather than simply visit, Joyce made a permanent home in the city for 20 years. It was in Paris that he secured publication of *Ulysses* as a single volume.

The influence of James Joyce on writers of the Lost Generation was so profound that it was almost a burden. The Irish novelist set the bar extremely high, despite having only a few published works under his belt. *Ulysses* became a blueprint for modern fiction. Specifically, the focus on interior monologue, mythological structures and irony were borrowed and copied by countless other writers in the 1920s and 1930s.

Sherwood Anderson: Dark Stories from Ohio

Sherwood Anderson was an enigmatic figure in American literature and a strong influence on the craft of fiction in the early 20th century. He was born in rural Ohio in 1876. Money trouble forced the family to move frequently. He joined the Army shortly before the Spanish-American War but never experienced combat. In his remarkable lifestyle, perhaps more so than his actual literary works, Sherwood Anderson provided inspiration to the young writers of the Lost Generation. In 1912, with a wife and children constituting a scene of apparent domestic bliss, Anderson suffered a mental breakdown and took to wandering the streets of Cleveland. He would later divorce his wife and abandon his family to pursue the creative life.

In 1919, he published *Winesburg, Ohio*, a collection of dark short stories that would be emulated by the younger generation. F. Scott Fitzgerald and T. S. Eliot both acknowledged that Anderson was a profound influence on their conception of the modern world. Anderson called the characters in his stories "grotesques." He continued writing short fiction and novels, but always fell short of the success of *Winesburg, Ohio*. Anderson frequently visited England and Europe but never settled into the expatriate lifestyle. Instead, he made a home and entertained literary guests, such as William Faulkner, in New Orleans. Nevertheless, Anderson's contributions to the Lost Generation and the avant-garde movements in the arts were substantial.

Ford Madox Ford: The Artist/Publisher

Born in 1873, the founder of *The Transatlantic Review* was a generation removed from the writers crowding the Latin Quarter of Paris. However, he was most certainly their compatriot in spirit. Ford Madox Ford grew up in privileged English family during the twilight of the Victorian era and absorbed the stately and proper literature of the period. He worked together with Joseph Conrad on the publication of several novels shortly after the turn of the century. Early in the war, Ford produced books for the British propaganda department. In 1915, at the age of 41, he volunteered for service in France. This act of bravery and patriotism, driven largely by his sense of duty, placed Ford into the shoes of men 20 years his junior. The experience had a deep and lasting effect on his politics and his art.

Ford's best-known work is *The Good Soldier*, a difficult and ambiguous work about two wealthy couples. The narrator admits uncertainty about details, revises facts and events throughout the novel, and claims knowledge about thoughts and feelings that he couldn't possibly have. In every sense, *The Good Soldier* is a Modernist novel and well ahead of its time. Even today, it's recognized as one of the finest examples of English literature from the war years.

In the context of the Lost Generation, Ford's most distinguished contribution was his founding of The Transatlantic Review. With this literary journal, Ford advanced the work of writers such as Hemingway, Joyce, Stein and Pound. He was instrumental in spreading the name of up-and-coming artists in America and Europe. In an ironic twist that didn't escape him, the fame of many of the writers he promoted would quickly surpass his own.

Chapter 5: Primary Representatives of the Lost Generation

Hemingway: The New Style

If one writer could be singled out as the model and the representative of the Lost Generation, that writer would be Ernest Hemingway. Born in Oak Park, Illinois, in 1899 to a respected and established family, Hemingway enjoyed a cultured upbringing. His mother was a musician, and his father practiced medicine. Later in life, Hemingway would distance himself from his mother. His biographers suggest that this was because they were so alike in temperament. As a youth, Hemingway enjoyed many of the same pursuits he would pursue as an adult: fishing, hunting, camping and simply being in nature.

Hemingway exemplified the new mode of thought and feeling and boldly rejected traditional, elaborate, "stuffy" literature. Hemingway had as profound and personal an experience of warfare as anyone in his social circle -- He served in the Italian ambulance service and survived devastating injuries in 1918. His youthful illusions about invincibility were dispelled at a young age. Hemingway's courtship with death would be a recurring theme throughout his life, as his interests would soon include bullfighting, the Running of the Bulls in Pamplona, and big game hunting in Africa. This courtship came to its logical conclusion in 1961, when he took his own life in Ketchum, Idaho. In 1920s Paris, Hemingway divided his energy between journalism and developing his writing talents.

The American novelist Sherwood Anderson convinced the Hemingway family – Ernest and his first wife, Hadley – that Paris was the ideal city in which to settle. He pointed to the low cost of living as well as the chance to hob-knob with some of the greatest artistic minds in the world. The Hemingways took Anderson's advice and moved to 74 Rue du Cardinal Lemoine in the Latin Quarter. Ernest worked as a foreign correspondent for the *Toronto Star Weekly*, submitting travel stories that foreshadowed his work in fiction. It was during this first sojourn in Paris that Hemingway befriended Gertrude Stein. Their relationship would later dissolve into bitter rivalry. However, in 1922, Stein immediately saw his talent and encouraged him to submit work for publication. By chance, Hemingway met Ezra Pound at Sylvia Beach's bookstore. The two initiated a friendship that would last for many years. Pound also introduced him to James Joyce, the Irish novelist. Hemingway was awed by these literary giants, but his relationships with Pound, Joyce and others only inspired him to ply his trade with even more diligence.

Hemingway's experience as a reporter informed his work as a storyteller. While a teenage reporter at the *Kansas City Star*, he absorbed the dictates of the paper's style guide, which stressed short, declarative sentences and active prose. As a combat journalist, he learned the necessity for extreme brevity in wire communications. He had to omit any needless words or phrases, distilling an idea to its sheer essence. This method of direct, clear and Spartan language would come to define the Hemingway style and spawn a flood of imitators. In 1925, his short story collection *In Our Time* was published. It was a revelation to readers on both sides of the Atlantic and garnered high praise from the critical establishment. Reviewers noted that the minimal, understated writing style had the effect of concentrating the emotional and thematic content of the stories. His inner circle of literary friends already knew something of his greatness, long before the rest of the world knew the name Ernest Hemingway.

Among the literati of Paris, Hemingway became an adored figure. To his friends, he was chivalrous and graceful. To his enemies, however, he could be a tyrannical bully. He was the image of strength and manliness, an image he worked hard to sustain. Hemingway's biographers have recorded the seething animosities that would eventually wreck many of his closest relationships and lead to three divorces. He was also a prolific drinker, but developed a reputation for his ability to drink heavily without showing obvious effects. He loved sports and outdoor activities, especially ones that emphasized strength and courage. Hemingway developed a strong appreciation for Spanish bullfighting and boxing, both of which he considered life and death struggles. His trauma during the war may have spurred him to seek out danger, testing his mettle time and again in order to feel alive.

Hemingway's relationship with fellow writer F. Scott Fitzgerald was among the most notable of his life, at least in terms of his literary development. Hemingway read and admired *The Great Gatsby*, which some suggest inspired him to begin work on his own novel. His friendship with Fitzgerald was intimate, but also troubled. Hemingway disliked Fitzgerald's effeminacy, self-consciousness and boorish behavior when drunk. When they first met, Hemingway believed he was in the presence of greatness. Later, when Fitzgerald was selling sub-par stories to magazines simply for the paycheck, Hemingway looked down on him as a fallen idol.

The Sun Also Rises was the novel that catapulted Hemingway onto the world literary stage. It was published by Scribner's in 1926, and some have argued that it represents his masterpiece. In one sense, *The Sun Also Rises* is an autobiography of the Lost Generation. Its characters are based on real people, and the events in the novel actually took place in Hemingway's life. The novel received mostly positive reviews. However, some only saw the story as a confirmation of the decadence and frivolity of the expatriate lifestyle. Hemingway strongly disagreed, arguing that his first novel upheld a sense of morality and celebrated a generation that survived a world war – with scars to show for it, but still in one piece.

F. Scott Fitzgerald: Class Consciousness

For the Fitzgerald family, the expatriate experience was far different from that of their contemporaries. They stopped only briefly in Paris in 1924 on their way to the French Riviera. The family was always on the move, regardless of whether Fitzgerald's income could support a lifestyle of luxury hotels, villas and lavish parties. It was Zelda, domineering and destructive throughout their marriage, who pushed her husband to write vapid stories for money and abandon his purely literary ambitions. To be fair, Fitzgerald himself had an unhealthy fixation of material luxury and upper-class respectability. In both his temperament and his aspirations, Fitzgerald was something of an outsider and an oddity among the literati of 1920s Paris.

In April 1925, the Fitzgeralds came to Paris and joined the approximately 30,000 other Americans living there at the time. However, instead of settling into the artistic community of the Left Bank (of the Seine River), the family rented an expensive apartment on the Right Bank. Unlike the Latin or Montparnasse Quarters, the Right Bank area of the city was the typical residence of wealthy tourists and business people. Fitzgerald simply didn't fit in with his generation, and he sensed as much. Part of him clung to the old traditions, where money and power equated to greatness, and little people were dispensable. The artist in him, though, saw the shallowness of such a belief system. Fitzgerald, therefore, suffered a constant internal struggle between his material wants and his artistic aspirations. Ultimately, the material side would come to dominate.

Despite his "fish out of water" status on the Left Bank, Fitzgerald did manage to forge several meaningful relationships with members of the more bohemian element. Most importantly, he rubbed elbows with both Ernest Hemingway and Gertrude Stein. However, his rampant drinking and attendant destructive behavior made many people avoid his company. He was known for drinking to excess and pulling nasty, mean-spirited practical jokes on people. Although he always felt remorse and begged forgiveness, Fitzgerald never seemed to gain the upper hand over his alcohol consumption. Nor did he gain control over his extravagant spending habits.

Had the Fitzgerald family practiced more restraint, money would never have been an issue. Fitzgerald's income from writing was more than enough to support the family reasonably well. Zelda and Scott had an affinity for lavish, expensive things and grand parties. His spending always kept pace with his income, such that the family never escaped a cycle of debt. Many of Fitzgerald's own life experiences can be seen in his stories. His tendency toward autobiography would be a handicap early in his career, but with the publication of *The Great Gatsby*, he had found the proper balance between personal and universal themes to craft a timeless and pitch-perfect narrative.

In writing *The Great Gatsby*, Fitzgerald no doubt owed a considerable debt to several artistic predecessors. Among these were T. S. Eliot and Joseph Conrad. Fitzgerald had a particular affinity for Conrad and tried to emulate the rich symbolism he saw in novels such as *Lord Jim* and *Heart of Darkness*. Similarly, he drew inspiration from Eliot's *The Waste Land*, seeing in that poem the rich complexity of ambiguous symbols, mythology and history. All of these influences coalesced within *The Great Gatsby*: astute readers recognize the ash-covered landscape that represents moral and physical decay, the watchful eyes of Dr. T. J. Eckleburg presiding over a dead world, and the light at the end of the Buchanans' pier that signifies the unattainable.

John Dos Passos: War and Politics

John Dos Passos was an illegitimate child, the son of a wealthy Midwestern lawyer. This facet of his birth and upbringing haunted him for much of his adult life. Despite his troubled childhood, Dos Passos received the kind of classical, literary education that was typical of young men growing up in privileged circumstances. He graduated Harvard in 1916 and left for Spain to study art. He felt compelled to contribute to the war effort and so joined the Norton-Harjes Ambulance Corps. The work took him to both Paris and Italy and provided material for his fiction during the 1920s. He enjoyed the company of Harvard classmates E. E. Cummings and Robert Hillyer in the ambulance corps. Cummings and Hillyer were both accomplished poets in their own right.

The work for which Dos Passos earned the highest praise came shortly after the war. In 1920, he finished *Three Soldiers*, an antiwar novel that is considered a classic of the genre. It has been favorably compared with *Red Badge of Courage*, another gritty war narrative from an earlier generation. Dos Passos spent most of the 1920s in Paris, but by the 1930s, his politics were changing. His friendship with Hemingway became strained during the Spanish Civil War. Dos Passos abhorred the tactics of the secret police, while Hemingway and others still believed in the power of a people's revolution. In hindsight, Dos Passos' political affiliation can best be described as libertarian. However, his firm rejection of pre-war European and American values assured his place as a member of the Lost Generation.

Waldo Peirce: Images of Life

Like Ernest Hemingway, Waldo Peirce drove an ambulance during the First World War. The French even awarded him with the Croix de Guerre for his actions at the Battle of Verdun. Also like Hemingway, Peirce was an imposing presence, with a tremendous laugh and a love for bawdy stories. Naturally, the two men became excellent friends in post-war Paris. Unlike most of Hemingway's relationships, the bond of affection with Peirce never soured.

Peirce was originally from Maine, born into a wealthy timber industry family. With the freedom to do as he wished, he chose to study painting and modern art. Although he attended Harvard College, it took him longer to graduate than usual, owing to his habit of frequenting pool halls. His paintings are typically categorized as Impressionist. He preferred landscapes, portraits and lively scenes, such as bars and bullfights. In post-war Paris and traveling with Hemingway, he would find ample inspiration for his canvas. On their many fishing trips in the Bahamas and Gulf of Mexico, Peirce would never be without his pencils and sketch pad.

The brawny painter from Maine befriended several other notable personalities during his stays in Paris. He was a frequent guest at Gertrude Stein's salon. He also became well acquainted with James Joyce, John Dos Passos, and Sylvia Beach and Bernice Abbott. Many of Peirce's paintings from this period offer intriguing visual glimpses into the spirit of the times. On the other hand, Peirce stood somewhat outside of the flow of Paris. Perhaps because he was a painter and not a writer, he didn't fit with the scene quite as well as some of his compatriots.

Unlike Hemingway, Peirce eventually became comfortable with family life and domestic stability. He returned to his native Maine and continued painting; some art critics suggest that, in later years, his productions lost their edge and became too regional. Peirce still went on the occasional fishing trip with his old friend, after settling in Maine he rarely wanted to go far away.

Kay Boyle: Sexual Politics and Proto-feminism

Kay Boyle was born in St. Paul, Minnesota and spent her youth in Cincinnati, Ohio. Unlike most women of her time, she had access to a quality education. Boyle studied architecture at Parsons in New York and violin at the Cincinnati Conservatory of Music. She was one of a handful of women to make her voice heard in the years after the Great War. Boyle married a French engineering student in the United States and relocated to France in 1923. She would spend much of the next 20 years living in various European countries, before returning to America in the 1940s.

In 1920s Paris, Boyle became intimate friends with many of the expatriate artists living on the Left Bank. She edited and wrote for several small literary magazines. The dominant themes of her poetry and fiction were the relationships between men and women in modern society, as well as the nature of love. Boyle was a feminist in an age when the word did not yet exist. She charted her own course and took her professional work seriously. It's unlikely that she would have had the same kind of life had she remained in America.

From an early age, Boyle had an aversion to war. At every opportunity, she expressed her opposition to armed conflict, in particular the Vietnam War. During the 1950s, Boyle and her husband drew the ire of Joseph McCarthy, and both were fired from their jobs and blacklisted. Her political activism was an inspiration to other throughout her life and was a sort of antidote to the sometimes self-absorbed fiction and poetry of the Lost Generation.

Hart Crane: Disillusioned, Defeated

Although he never faced combat, Harold Hart Crane's brief life is still one of tragedy and unfulfilled promise. He committed suicide at the age of 32 by jumping from a steamer into the Gulf of Mexico. His despair was a combination of several factors: the perceived failure of his artistic career, his drinking problems and his homosexuality. Whereas other gay and lesbian artists were able to embrace their sexual identities, Crane would always struggle. For much of the 1920s, he sought venues to showcase his work in a variety of small literary magazines.

The publication of *White Buildings* in 1926, a collection of thoroughly Modernist verse, earned Crane much-deserved recognition. Crane saw his mission as being an antidote to the dark pessimism of T. S. Eliot, in particular *The Waste Land*. Eliot's work, therefore, both inspired him and challenged him. For years, in between bouts of poverty and heavy drinking, he worked on his next poem. With the help of friends, *The Bridge* was finally published in 1930. Like most of his verse, the poem is dense, difficult and full of irony. Most of the reviews, however, were negative. Crane's difficulty in establishing his own identity in a rapidly changing world is emblematic of the plight of the Lost Generation. Only years after his death was his poetic genius recognized and applauded.

Erich Maria Remarque: The German Experience

Fighting for his native Germany during the war, Erich Maria Remarque experienced the same sense of tragedy and hopelessness by the conclusion of hostilities. His war experience created in him a strong belief in pacifism, a belief that would later land him in trouble with Nazi German authorities. During the Second World War, Remarque barely escaped Germany with his life; his sister, Elfriede Sholz, was not so lucky. Sholz was convicted in a kangaroo court and executed on December 16, 1943.

Remarque, like many of his generation, was a rambler. The war experience unmoored him from his homeland, both physically and philosophically. His most celebrated literary contribution was *All Quiet on the Western Front*, a novel about the wartime experiences of a common German soldier. The novel portrays the futility and hardship of war, as well as the difficulty of returning to civilian life after years spent in the trenches. In many ways, *All Quiet on the Western Front* anticipated the experience of war veterans throughout the century. The sense of "you can't go home again" resonates throughout Remarque's work after the war, and positions him firmly as a member of the Lost Generation.

Chapter 6: Critical Reception

Newspapers and magazines did not always paint a favorable portrait of the expatriates in France. Many news outlets reported that the Latin Quarter of Paris, epicenter of the artistic community, was home to decadence and depravity. From the perspective of conservative Americans, the label may have been accurate, however exaggerated the truth might have been. Some also believed that putting down stakes in a foreign country was unpatriotic. That stance ignores the fact that many of the themes and topics in the writings of the Lost Generation were thoroughly American. Many of the expatriates in Paris believed that crossing the Atlantic gave them a perspective on their homeland that could not be achieved otherwise. It would be inaccurate to say that the English-speaking residents of Paris had low opinions of their places of origin.

The critical reviews of the Lost Generation's artistic productions range from glowing to hostile. The tone of the reviews depended largely on the political and social stance of the reviewer in question. Conservative critics found plenty to dislike in the work of Hemingway or T. S. Eliot. The abandonment of Victorian aesthetics was seen as a sacrilege. In particular, Hemingway's simplistic style, with its short, declarative sentences, was sometimes compared unfavorably with children's literature. James Joyce may have received the strongest condemnation of all: His Ulysses was burned in New York City, and the book was outlawed nationwide. Little wonder that so many creative minds sought the freedom and escape of a more permissive environment.

Chapter 7: Essential Reading List

T. S. Eliot (1888-1965)

The Waste Land, 1922

> Eliot's long-form poem is probably the
> landmark for a certain kind of
> modernist literature, one that
> recognizes futility and despair. The
> poem employs multiple points of view
> and styles to build a coherent image of
> a broken, fallen world.

Ezra Pound (1885-1972)

Hugh Selwyn Mauberley, 1920

The 18 individual poems that make up *Hugh Selwyn Mauberley* are part autobiography and part satire. Pound's self-deprecation, humor and willingness to abandon conventions signaled a transition in his work as a poet, away from tradition and toward experimentation.

Gertrude Stein (1874-1946)

The Autobiography of Alice B. Toklas, 1933

Toklas' autobiography is unquestionably Stein's autobiography. The unusual and ironic use of a false perspective, deliberately bending the meaning of the autobiographical form, is a decidedly modernist approach. The narrative offers one of the most complete glimpses of life in Paris and of the Stein salons.

James Joyce (1882-1941)

Ulysses, 1922

Joyce's masterpiece takes place in a single day, in Dublin. The structure, themes and characters in the novel echo the classical mythology of The Odyssey. The novel continues to be a powerful influence and inspiration.

Sherwood Anderson (1876-1941)

Winesburg, Ohio, (1919)

The subtitle for Anderson's crowning achievement is "A Group of Tales of Ohio Small-Town Life." The bleakness of the scenery and the characters would be a strong influence on fiction writing throughout the 1920s and 1930s.

Ford Madox Ford (1873-1939)

The Good Soldier, 1915

This unconventional narrative, with plenty of ambiguity and shifting perspectives, was ahead of its time. The novel follows two wealthy but morally damaged couples through pre-war Europe. The influence of Joseph Conrad is powerful, but *The Good Soldier* is a unique work of fiction.

Ernest Hemingway (1899-1961)

In Our Time, 1925

This collection of short stories and vignettes announced Hemingway's presence as a talent of the first order. The stories are short and elegant, clearly betraying his journalistic influences. They include fishing stories and bullfighting stories and cover the range of human emotion.

The Sun Also Rises, 1926

Hemingway's first novel is a portrait of the expatriate way of life in France. The characters and events are all based in real life, and the novel's themes include hope, pain, recovery, trust and morality.

A Moveable Feast, 1964

> Published posthumously, Hemingway's memoirs of life in Paris during the 1920s offer an intriguing, if biased, glimpse into the lives and personalities of fellow artists such as Gertrude Stein, F. Scott Fitzgerald, James Joyce and John Dos Passos. The work is well known for its biting sarcasm and humor, both of which border on mean-spirited.

F. Scott Fitzgerald (1896-1940)

The Great Gatsby, 1925

> *The Great Gatsby* is a nuanced and insightful portrait of the shallow, decadent life that money so often creates. The novel is remarkable for its complexity and rich symbolism, all contained in a relatively slim volume.

Tender is the Night, 1934

Fitzgerald's fourth and final novel, *Tender is the Night* is crucial for the way it represents the degeneration of people in the wake of the roaring twenties. The novel closely mirrors life, as his own life and relationship with Zelda was deteriorating at the time, not to mention Zelda's mental health.

H. D. (Hilda Doolittle) (1886-1961)

Sea Garden, 1916

H. D. belonged to the Imagist school of poetry and was initially inspired by Ezra Pound. Her first collection of poetry, *Sea Garden*, is quintessentially Imagistic, with lots of unexpected rhythms and imagery.

E. E. Cummings (1894-1962)

The Enormous Room, 1922

Cummings spent four months wrongly imprisoned during the First World War. He recounted these experienced in his first novel, while also showing off his characteristic narrative and punctuation style. *The Enormous Room* was inspirational to many Lost Generation writers.

Hart Crane (1899-1932)

White Buildings, 1926

With *White Buildings*, Crane rejects both the lyrical and the language poetry traditions and charts his own course. Many argue that, were it not for his suicide at 32, he would be acknowledged as one of the greatest American poets of the century.

John Dos Passos

***Three Soldiers*, 1920**

Dos Passos drew upon his experience as an ambulance driver to craft this compelling war story. *Three Soldiers* is an unromantic look at the reality of the Great War and one of the best American war novels of the era.

Djuna Barnes (1892-1982)

Nightwood, 1936

None other than T. S. Eliot wrote a glowing introduction to this semiautobiographical novel of Parisian life in the 1920s. The themes of sexual exploration and societal values were at the time revolutionary and pushed the boundaries of acceptable fiction.

Kay Boyle (1902-1992)

Short Stories, 1929

Boyle's fiction cleverly explores the struggle to define oneself as a woman in a world dominated by men. Her early work won two O. Henry Awards, the most prestigious prize for short fiction in America.

Edmund Wilson (1895-1972)

Axel's Castle: A Study in the Imaginative Literature of 1870-1930, 1931

> This work of literary criticism examines the roots and development of symbolism in modern literature, including the work of James Joyce. Wilson was a classmate of F. Scott Fitzgerald at Princeton and the two were excellent friends.

Erich Maria Remarque (1898-1970)

All Quiet on the Western Front, 1929

> Remarque's novel of trench warfare from the German perspective reveals that the experience of soldiers in the war was universally terrible. The novel's antiwar sentiments later get him into trouble with Nazi authorities.

Archibald MacLeish (1892-1982)

Einstein, 1929

This long-form, experimental poem exhibited all the traits of modernism. MacLeish was known for lending aid to fellow artists more so than for his own work, but *Einstein* demonstrates that he was a first-rate poet.

References

Aldridge, John. *After the Lost Generation*. New York:
McGraw-Hill, 1951. Print.

Baker, Carlos. *Ernest Hemingway: A Life Story*. New
York: Scribners, 1969. Print.

Cowley, Malcolm. *A Second Flowering*. New York:
Viking Press, 1956. Print.

Durham, Carolyn A. "Modernism and Mystery: The
Curious Case of the Lost Generation."
Twentieth-Century Literature 49.1 (2003): pp.
82-102. Print.

Field, Allyson Nadia. "Expatriate Lifestyle as Tourist
Destination: *The Sun Also Rises* and
Experiential Travelogues of the Twenties."
The Hemingway Review 25.2 (2006): pp. 29-
43. Print.

Fitch, Noel Riley. *Sylvia Beach and the Lost
Generation*. New York: Norton, 1983. Print.

Hovis, George. "Beyond the Lost Generation: The Death of Egotism in *You Can't Go Home Again*." *The Thomas Wolfe Review* 33.1 (2009): pp. 32-37. Print.

"Literary Expatriates in Paris." *UNC University Libraries*. Web. 10 July 2012.

Mellow, James. *Charmed Circle: Gertrude Stein & Company*. New York: Praeger, 1974. Print.

Putnam, Samuel. *Paris Was Our Mistress*. New York: Viking Press, 1947. Print.

Soto, Michael. "Hemingway Among the Bohemians: A Generational Reading of *The Sun Also Rises*." *The Hemingway Review* 21.1 (2001): pp. 5-21. Print.

Vincent, Jonathan. "'Tendrils of Association': World War I Narrative and the U.S. Political Imaginary." *American Literature* 82.3 (2010): pp. 554-581. Print.

18750908R00043

Printed in Great Britain
by Amazon